How to be a Ventriloquist

by

Darren Griffin

To my wife and children and all those who believe.

Table of contents

Introduction

When I was young (first grade and second grade) I dabbled in magic. It has always fascinated me and I joined a mail order magic club which sent me a new trick every month.

I thought that becoming a "Master of Magic" would add spark to an otherwise dull existence.

What it added was failure. I was (and still am) a horrible magician. All the preparation and practice, needing the audience's eyes to be in a certain spot at a certain time, never came together for me. I did shows for the class but the tricks that worked in my room in front of the mirror somehow melted down in front of a live audience. Consistently. I mean every single time!

This path was not my destiny.

Then I found REAL MAGIC.

It was November and I was eight years old. Back then department stores would mail out big fat catalogs full of toys and games of every kind and included full-color pictures above their descriptions. Armed with a magic marker, I turned page after page looking for items worthy of circling. You see, somehow, through the magic of the season, a circled item could turn into the actual item on Christmas morning. It was also important to show the circled items to my mother, although I never knew why. After pages of race cars, building blocks, and (of all things) clothes, I found a page dedicated to ventriloquist dummies. I was intrigued. I was familiar with ventriloquism because my dad collected old radio programs. The faces of the characters gazed at me from the page. "This is what you want for Christmas" floated through my brain.

I passed the catalogs through the usual channels, and after an ETERNITY of waiting (time passes much slower when you're a kid), Christmas day finally came. Under the tree was an eight-year-old sized rocking chair (nice, but I hadn't asked for it) and in the chair was . . . (drum roll) a ventriloquist dummy! Santa had come through! Next to him was a record with lessons on how to speak without moving your lips. It also contained some practice scripts. I devoured it. I listened to it over and over and practiced, and practiced, and practiced. The dummy, whose name was Danny, and I became best friends and I became the only ventriloquist in the third grade. I was even asked to do a few shows for the class.

These shows did NOT melt down! No hidden cards, no strings up my sleeve, just Danny and I anywhere, anytime. We got laughs! Not the laughs you get when you blow a magic trick, but real honest laughter.

You're thinking "OK, how is this REAL MAGIC?"

I'm glad you asked.

Ventriloquism (pronounced ven-TRIL-o-kwism) uses the two most powerful kinds of real magic that everyone has inside them.

YOUR

VOICE

and

your

imagination

(How's that for an over the top graphic?)

Everyone has a voice and hopefully an imagination. When you combine the two you create a world without limits that is uniquely yours. Imagine a world where anything around you can talk and have a personality. Now you've got the idea.

This book is designed to teach you all you need to know about being a great ventriloquist. Whether it becomes a hobby or a profession you will bring laughter and magic to your life and the lives of those around you.

Chapter 1

The History

You probably knew that ventriloquism has been around for quite a while, but did you know that the earliest record we have of the use of ventriloquism comes from ancient Greece?

The Greeks built a temple to Apollo in a place called Delphi in the sixth century B.C. They believed that Apollo would speak to them through his "oracle", a human chosen by the gods to relay their words to the people. In this case it was a priestess named Pythia. Pythia would stand as if in a trance, mouth unmoving, as the words of Apollo came from within the temple, or out of the sky or maybe from a sacred stone.

Yup, she was a ventriloquist.

The Greeks called the ability "Gastromancy", referring to the use of the diaphragm to project the voice without moving the lips. I am really glad we don't use the term today. "Hi I'm Darren and I'm a gastromancer!" Sounds like some type of stomach trouble.

The origin of the word "ventriloquism" is a combination of two Latin words: "Ventre" (the belly) and "Loqui" (to speak). A belly speaker.

Many shamans and witch doctors used the technique to allow the "spirits of the dead" or the "ancient ancestors" to speak to the villagers.

Ventriloquism became popular in our culture during the early 1900s with a form of entertainment called "Vaudeville". This was a stage show with jugglers, comics, singers and dancers, and ventriloquists. This was pure entertainment where the ventriloquist would talk to a "dummy" (they prefer the word "figure") or an animal puppet. They would "throw their voice" under the stage or from a trunk. Their "dummy" would sing while the ventriloquist drank a glass of water or lit and puffed on a cigarette (not recommended, I only smoke if I'm on fire).

From Vaudeville it spread to radio, film and eventually television. You may have seen modern ventriloquists on TV.

Some of them even write books on how to be a ventriloquist. The very idea.

Chapter 2

How The Heck Does It Work?

Now we start getting to the good stuff.

Part of the magic of ventriloquism comes from keeping your lips still while you speak. In order to keep your lips from moving you will need to learn the "Ventriloquist's Alphabet", the letters that can be said without moving your lips.

First, however, let's talk about the position of the mouth. If you can sit in front of a mirror for this part so much the better. A mirror is really the key to developing a still mouth.

Take a moment and go find one you can sit in front of. I'll wait.

♪♪ La de da, La la tum te tum ♫

Got one? Not yet. OK.

♫Doobee doo ♪

Welcome back. Ok, the correct position of the mouth. Smile comfortably. Just a pleasant smile, lips slightly apart with your front teeth lightly touching. Don't grit your teeth and smile insanely as if you were a great white shark who just stumbled across a surfer party. Just a pleasant, comfortable smile. Lips slightly apart with your teeth lightly touching.

It should look natural, not forced. Look in the mirror. Looks natural? Well done.

Now that your mouth is in the proper position here are the letters you can say without moving your lips. The other letters, the ones you can't say without movement, we'll get to shortly.

The Ventriloquist's Alphabet

A C D E G H I

J K L N O Q

R S T U X Z

The letters you CAN say
without moving your lips!

Go ahead, give it a try. Mouth in the proper position.

No really, stop reading and give it a whirl. You may be surprised at how well you do this first time.

How'd it go? Remember the key to being a great ventriloquist is PRACTICE PRACTICE PRACTICE in front of the mirror. Try it a few more times until you feel comfortable with it.

When you're ready to move on, I'll be right here.

Chapter 3

The Other Letters

These are the ones that just can't be said without moving the lips. This is also the "Great Secret" of ventriloquism. After reading this you will never look at ventriloquism the same.

OK, enough of the dramatic buildup. Here they are.

The Other Letters

B F M P
V W Y

The letters you CAN'T say
without moving your lips!

So how do we get around this? By using
SUBSTITUTIONS.

What does it mean to "substitute"? In this case it
means replacing the letter with another one that

sounds kind of like it from the Ventriloquist's Alphabet list.

"What madness is this?" you ask.

Believe me, it really works. By using substitutions you will be able to say anything you want while keeping your lips rock steady.

B becomes D

F becomes ETH

M becomes N

P becomes T

V becomes THE

W is a little complicated. It becomes OH. I'll explain in a minute.

As for Y it's only the sound of the letter itself that is hard to say. For Y say OH-EYE fast.

The trick is to say the substitution but think the actual letter. Say F but think ETH.

In order to master these substitutions here are some practice exercises. Don't be surprised if they sound a little strange at first. That's to be expected. In a way you're learning a new language, or re-learning how to speak. Be patient with yourself. Remember to keep your mouth in the correct position. Don't forget to practice in front of the mirror.

Chapter 4

Exercises

The letter B.

Practice sentence: The Boy Brought a Balloon.

(Remember the substitution for B is D.)

Practice saying: The Doy Drought a Daloon.

Sounds funky right? Not to worry.

Here's a tip no one thought to share with me. Maybe no one else has thought of it, who knows.

When you say these substitutions notice where your tongue is in your mouth.

Notice that "The Doy Drought a Daloon" causes you to put the tip of the tongue on the roof of your mouth when you make the D sound. Now try this. Say "The Doy Drought a Dalloon" but touch the tip of the tongue to the area where your front teeth are touching. In other words, when you make the D sound have your tongue touching your front teeth right where they are touching each other. This gives it a softer sound, and makes the substitution sound even more believable.

Now if this doesn't sound absolutely perfect you're right on track. It won't for a while. After practicing every day you will begin to notice that it sounds better and better. Repeat it in front of the mirror 4 or 5 more times. This is the most difficult letter and takes time to perfect. Don't worry about how it sounds; just make sure you are keeping your lips still. That's the important part right now.

Remember that when you do a show or write a script you would never use a sentence like "The boy brought a balloon". You might say something like "Yesterday I saw a balloon". The substitution will blow by the audience so quickly they will never notice it. Remember that people hear what they expect to hear. If you have seen a ventriloquist before you've heard these substitutions, but never noticed them. Don't be discouraged; just keep up the practice, practice, practice.

The letter F.

This one's a lot easier.

Remember the substitution for F is ETH. Sounds like F but doesn't require moving your lips.

Practice sentence: Frank Followed a Feline.

Practice saying: THrank THollowed a THeline.

Keep your mouth in the proper position and practice in front of your mirror. Looks good doesn't it?

The letter M.

The substitution for M is N.

Practice sentence: Monsters Make Me Mad.

Practice saying: Nonsters Nake Ne Nad.

Don't forget to put the tip of your tongue right behind your teeth, right where they touch.

The letter P.

The substitution for P is T.

Practice sentence: Pete Plays the Piano.

Practice saying: Tete Tlays the Tiano.

The letter V.

The substitution for V is THE.

Practice sentence: Virginia Values a Vast Victory.

Practice saying: THirginia THalues a THast THictory.

The letter W.

W is a bit wonky, but easy.

Let's take the word "Why". With your mouth in the proper position say "OH-EYE". Now say it faster. Even faster. Faster! You go! If you say it fast enough it will sound like "Why". This is also the way to say the letter "Y". The sound that Y makes is easy to say with still lips, it's only the name of the letter that needs a substitution.

Practice sentence: Where were we walking?

Practice saying: OH-ere OH-uhr OH-ee OH-alking?

Don't forget to say the substitution really fast, until it sounds like the actual word. Don't say the whole sentence fast or no one will be able to understand you. Just run the OH into the rest of the word quickly to get the W sound.

The letter Y.

There is no exercise for Y, as I mentioned it's only the name of the letter itself that's hard to say. Say OH-EYE quickly to make the Y.

Remember to keep your lips in the correct position: comfortable smile, lips slightly apart, front teeth lightly touching. Practice in front of the mirror.

Even though these exercises sound a bit strange, once you are used to using the substitutions you can use them in regular conversation and the audience won't even notice. They hear what they expect to hear.

Nifty huh?

Chapter 5

Creating a Character

Now that you have all the letters handled and can speak without moving your lips, it's time to decide what type of voice to use for your character. There are three basic types.

Basic Types of Voices

1. Falsetto
A high pitched voice.
(Sounds like a certain
cartoon mouse)

2. Mid Range
A voice pitched SLIGHTLY
higher than your own.

3. Lower Register
A voice pitched lower
than your own.

Experiment with each type of voice and see which
you like the best for creating your first character.
Then go back and practice the alphabet and the
substitutions in this new voice. Practice switching

between your voice and your characters voice. It's no longer necessary to keep your lips still when using your own voice, your lips are supposed to move when you are speaking. It's only when using your character's voice that your lips need to be still. This gives the illusion that your character is speaking and not you.

As you are creating your character, put as much detail into their personality as you can. The more real he or she is to you the more real they will be to the audience. Making a character profile can be useful.

Character Profile

NAME. Pretty self explanatory. You want a name that reflects their personality as much as possible. A farmer might be named "Isaac" or "Clem" or something like that. A dragon could be "Sparky". There are lots of sites on line that will give you lists of names.

AGE. A character that is young will be very different than an old one. They will have different interests. A youth will have stories about school, playing outside. An older character will talk about their job, kids, rush hour, air planes. A fantasy character (dragon, wizard things like that) could be any age. Even hundreds of years old.

VOICE. Use a voice that matches your character. A small one would have a high voice. A large one would have a lower voice.

BIOGRAPHY. Their life story. Where were they born? Large family? Small? Do they live in a city or the country? Pets?

PERSONALITY. Are they happy, grumpy? Friendly, cheerful, honest or dishonest? Goofy or serious? Optimistic? Think about people you know and their personality traits. Make your character as interesting as you can.

LIKES AND DISLIKES. What do they enjoy? What do they hate? Do they have a pet peeve? Love ice cream or pizza? Hate math?

BEST QUALITIES. What are their strengths? What do they do well or are good at? What can be admired about them? Intelligence, honesty, imagination, physical abilities?

WORST QUALITIES. What are their weaknesses? Are they tempted to shop lift, lie? Are they kinda stupid? Don't feel this will make a character the audience won't like. We all have things that tempt us and your character will be all the more real by having these weaknesses. Maybe you can have a conversation with them about how they can overcome their problems.

OCCUPATION. What do they do during the day? Are they old enough to have a job or do they go to school? Are they a farmer, fireman, astronaut, ballet dancer, opera singer?

HOBBIES AND TALENTS. Do they play piano or sing? Collect comic books, watch television, go to movies? Do they paint, read, play games?

The more you flesh out your character the more real they will be to the audience.

Chapter 6

Figures and Puppets

Now you need to make sure that the voice and personality matches how your character actually looks.

One of the benefits of being a ventriloquist is that you can make anything talk. Many use puppets, which are usually very affordable and can be found in toy stores or on line.

Others use a professional figure, or "dummy". These usually cost several hundred dollars.

I use both figures and puppets in my shows.

You can use sock puppets, paper bag puppets, even paint your hand. It is not necessary to spend much or any money on your characters.

Practice holding conversations with your new friend in front of the mirror. Just chat and see what comes up. This is where you get material for your show. Since you have a character profile, you can imagine what they would say or do in most situations. Just have fun with it and see what comes out.

Chapter 7

Final Words

As I said earlier, this is REAL MAGIC. Use your imagination to create a character and your voice to bring it to life. Create your own world where handkerchiefs talk, animals crack jokes and everything around you is funny and friendly. There are no limits to your imagination, and anything you can imagine you can make live. Show your audience things they've never seen before.

Most of all have fun!

Printed in Great Britain
by Amazon

59631456R00023